Hollywood's Rising Stars Monologues

Ages 4-18

JOANNE MOSCONI

Edited by Joan Mosconi
Cover design by John Piano
Interior Design by Asya Blue
Copyright © 2020 Joanne Mosconi
All rights reserved.
First Edition: March 2020

ISBN: 978-1-7341257-2-6
E book 978-1-7341257-3-3

DEDICATION

I dedicate this book to all young people who have the ability to dream big, and to all the little ones in my life who inspired these monologues.

This book would not exist without the help, passion and support of so many wonderful people.

A special thank you to my mother **Joan Mosconi**, who is the best teacher I know and who helped me edit this book. My creative husband, **John Piano,** who designed the cover of this book and encouraged me to write it. **Asya Blue**, my book designer, thank you for being such an incredible talent and making my book beautiful. **My acting students**, without you this book would not be possible. Our lessons inspired every piece.

> *"Today you are you! That is truer than true!*
> *There is no one alive who is you-er than you!"*
> ~ Dr. Seuss

TABLE OF CONTENTS

INDEX

TITLE	CHARACTER	GENDER	GENRE	PAGE
The American Girl Doll	Mikayla	F	Comedy	57
All I Want for Christmas	Vince/Veronica	M/F	Drama	59
Dogs Go to Heaven Too	Angelo/Arabella	M/F	Drama	61
AGES 12-15				
The Cell Phone	Soh/Sing	M/F	Comedy	67
Like Like Like Like You	Marina	F	Comedy	69
Will You Be My Sister?	Donna	F	Drama	71
I am Not Neurotic, I'm Smart!	Angelina	F	Comedy	74
Mean Girls	Amalia	F	Drama	78
Not Ready to Say Goodbye	Koda/Kylie	M/F	Drama	81
Homework is a Waste of Time	Ryder	M	Comedy	84
You Can't Quit	Belle	F	Drama	87
The Monnors	Connor	M	Comedy	89
Worried About Mom	Jake	M	Drama	91
AGES 16-18				
The Diary	Meg	F	Drama	95
YouTube Star	Amy	F	Comedy	98
Gelato, Please!	Brenda	F	Comedy	101
The Prom Dress	Tammy	F	Dramedy	106
The Promise Ring	Blake	M	Drama	110
Where is God?	Mark/Mila	M/F	Drama	113
I'm Screwed	Steve	M	Comedy	115
The Genie	Cole	M	Comedy	117
Too Shy	Keith	M	Comedy	119
My Mother's New Boyfriend	Chris	M/F	Drama	122

INTRODUCTION

Monologues! You know what those are. Those long speeches said by a solo actor on stage or on the big screen. Yup, those things! So you want to be an actor, but you hate learning and performing monologues, is that right? If that's so, think again. Monologues are very important for both your training and career as an actor.

When I first start coaching a new client, I always tell them that I would like to work with them on both a dramatic and a comedic monologue. This is how we start off our training. However, if you are serious about a career in acting, I recommend that you constantly learn new monologues and have at least 4 different ones ready at any given time. You never know when you might need them.

Award winning Acting Coach, Larry Moss says: *"I'm a believer in monologues simply because they're good when you're by yourself, as a workout, daily. I say, you must have four monologues ready to go at all times."*

The reason why I emphasize the importance of monologues is that they are not only an amazing piece to have on hand for a performance, but they serve as an excellent training tool as well. Actors get the opportunity to discover new choices for their characters the more they rehearse their pieces. Also, having a performance ready monologue helps the actor prepare for anything and everything. Let's say you just nailed an audition, but the casting director wants to see more-*Perform your monologue for them*! If you need something submitted by tape, and need it ASAP- *Perform your monologue!* Your monologue provides you with the opportunity to showcase your work.

Monologues are an important piece to include in your acting toolbox, especially when you are starting your career. If you are searching for your first agent or manager, a monologue may be the only way for them to see your work. The goal is to eventually have an acting reel, which will showcase your work. But until you have work to show, auditioning with monologues will be critical early on.

Here is my golden advice- Most actors are not willing to do the work to nail their monologues. If you want to be different and stand out, do not fake your preparation.

Prepare your monologues as if it is the most important thing you do as an actor. It will only help you, I promise.

HOW TO USE THIS BOOK

As a top acting coach in both Los Angeles and NYC, I know what kinds of monologues young actors need. The best part about the monologues I created in this book is that they are just for young people like you.

1. AGE APPROPRIATE:
I have divided the book into different age groups, so be sure to turn to the section for your specific age. Select a piece that fits your age. This means you must know your type. Knowing your type will help you rock your auditions. I want you to read all the monologues for your age group and then choose the one you relate to the most.

Please note that many of the pieces are gender neutral, but for those that are not, please feel free to change a male's monologue to a female's monologue or vice versa.

2. THE INVISIBLE OTHER PERSON:
Each character in this book is talking to someone else, the "invisible other person." Make sure you establish who that person is when you are rehearsing. They are just as important to the piece as you are. One of the reasons that motivated me to write my own monologue book is I found myself constantly displeased with some of the monologues my young actors would choose to work on. Many of these monologues would have a character just sharing a story.

I want young people to avoid these. Why? There is not enough action in this kind of piece to really showcase your abilities. Instead, I wrote monologues where the character is talking to someone else and has something at stake. This kind of monologue allows for a performance that will be more alive. It will allow you, the rising star, to be active as you fight for what you want in the moment.

3. REHEARSAL QUESTIONS:

At the end of each monologue, I ask you 5 questions. Carefully answer each one. They will help you connect to the piece and prepare for the role. These are questions I ask my own students when working on a monologue.

4. DIRECTOR'S TIP:

I also have provided you with a director's tip at the end of each monologue for you to consider while you rehearse. Check out all my director's tips in the book and see which ones you can apply to your rehearsal process.

5. REHEARSAL:

I recommend that you rehearse your monologue daily and even perform it for your friends and family so that you can get used to doing it live. The monologues I wrote for you are based on true stories I have heard through the years from working with young people. They are perfect to use for auditions, acting classes, performances, or just for fun with your friends.

6. ENTERTAIN US:

Your job as an actor is to entertain us. *I know, can you believe it?* Each of the monologues in this book has a clear story-with a beginning, middle and end. I recommend dividing it into these three sections. You must be able to tell the story through the choices you make.

7. 60 SECONDS:

Each of these monologues are 60 seconds or less, with an exception of a few. Feel free to cut down any monologue that is running over 60 seconds. Why do I recommend 60 seconds? If you can catch your audience's attention in 60 seconds or less and entertain them, it is much more effective than boring them for two minutes or more. Less is more, always!

8. CONNECT:

Are you connected to the monologue you chose? If not, why do it? I love when my actors see themselves in their monologues. It will help you access the truth behind your words. If you're connected, then we will be too. If you are not connected, no one will be. Keep this in mind as you hunt for your next piece so you can *BOOK THE JOB!*

BREAK A LEG RISING STARS!

Follow Joanne Mosconi on Instagram
@theperformingartscoach and on her website at
www.theperformingartscoach.com

Hollywood's Rising Stars Monologues

AGES 4-7

RED CAR

Pietro is frustrated that his mom will not buy him a new toy. Usually when he cries a lot, his mother gives in, but today she will not budge. This makes Pietro wildly upset.

Mama, I want the red car. *(whining)* NO! I don't already have one. Fine, then I want a blue car. Actually, I want a yellow car, like that taxi cab we were in yesterday. Why can't you buy me one? *(begins crying)* I don't want to eat my pasta! I don't want broccoli. I want you to buy me a car! Fine, then I am not going to EAT! NO! Don't call dad and tell him. Then he won't take me to the park. Please Mama! Don't call him. Please! I promise to eat all my pasta. Yes, and my broccoli too. *(He begins eating.)* Maybe Daddy will buy me a red car!

REHEARSAL DISCUSSION:

1. What is Pietro feeling during this monologue? Why is he feeling this way?

2. Do you think Pietro should get the car from his mom? Why or why not?

3. Why does Pietro not want to eat his pasta or broccoli?

4. Why does he change his mind and eat his food, even though at first he does not want to?

5.   What does Pietro want from his mother? Does he get it?

DIRECTOR'S TIP:

Have fun exploring all the emotions Pietro experiences in this monologue. In the beginning try playing the scene whining, and then allow yourself to get frustrated in the middle. By the end, try something different, like begging your mom to not call your dad because you don't want to get in trouble. Have fun exploring all the choices you can make for Pietro. How will you say your last line? Try different ways and then choose the strongest choice.

BATMAN COSTUME

Donnie is dressed like Batman, and this makes his older brother Chris upset since Donnie is always Robin. This time Donnie wants to change the rules!

I am not taking off my Batman costume. Mom bought it for me and she said that I can be Batman too. How come every time we play, I have to be Robin? Why can't you be him today? So what if you're older than me. I don't care if Batman is taller than Robin! This is make believe Chris. *(Pretending to be Batman)* " I am going to rescue the people of New York from The Joker who is in The Empire State Building keeping them trapped. You can come and help me Robin!" Hey, Chris! Where are you going? Don't leave! Can I come and play with you and your friends too? Why not? Chris, come back! I can be Robin and you can be Batman. Robin is way cooler than Batman anyway.

REHEARSAL DISCUSSION:

1. What does Donnie want from his brother Chris in this monologue?

2. Why is it hard for Donnie to get what he wants from Chris?

3. Do you have a brother or sister? Are you the oldest or the youngest?

4. Can you relate to Donnie or Chris? Explain why.

5. Why do you think Donnie decides to be Robin at the end of the monologue?

DIRECTOR'S TIP:

Watch a few Batman and Robin episodes to get you into character. This is a piece for a super hero fan.

CRYING IN THE SKY

Paolo/Paula is walking home from school with his/her Madrina. (Madrina translates to Godmother in Spanish.) Madrina's beloved dog, Match, died a month ago. On the walk home from school, it begins to rain.

Madrina, I miss Match. She used to make this funny noise every time she wanted something. It went like this *(Paolo/Paola demonstrates for Madrina the noise Match made with enthusiasm.) Grrrrrrrrrrr… Grrrrrrrrrrr.* Even though it sounded like she was being mean, we knew she was just talking to us, right?

(Paolo/Paola points to the sky) Hey look, Match is crying. Anytime water falls from the sky, I know it's her tears. Loretta told me that it's just rain, but I know what it really is. When Match went to the sky, she started crying a lot up there. Maybe it's because she wants to go on a walk and nobody understands her *Grrrrrrrrrrr* like the way we do.

Madrina, why are you crying? Is it because you miss Match too? Will you ever go up to the sky to see Match? I know you miss her, but please don't go anytime soon. Ever since Mama told me that Match went to the sky, Match never came back, and I want you with us. If you miss her, do what I do. Catch one of her tears and tell her you love her. Watch! *(Paolo/Paola catches a rain drop and looks up to the sky.)*

Stop crying Match, because we love you so much. Madrina and I miss you, but we know we will see you again one day soon.

See, it works. No more water is falling!

REHEARSAL DISCUSSION:

1. What is Paolo/Paola feeling during this monologue? Why is he/she feeling this way?

2. Do you think Paolo/Paola is close to his/her Madrina? Why or why not? How does he/she react when Madrina starts crying?

3. What does it mean that Match went to the sky?

4. Where and When does this scene take place?

5. Next time it rains, go outside and experience it. How does the rain smell? What does the sky look like? What does the rain sound like as it falls from the sky? What does the rain taste like? What does rain feel like as it hits your face? Now, the next time you rehearse this scene, make sure Paolo/Paola experiences the rain drops. This monologue will stand out if the actor creates the rain and experiences it as it falls from the sky.

DIRECTOR'S TIP:

When Paolo/Paola imitates Match's *Grrrrrrrrrr*, have fun

with this. Really pretend to act like a dog and take your time. Keep in mind, Match was part of their family, so there is a lot of love for this beloved pet. During rehearsal, imagine you are talking to your aunt and actually imagine her when Madrina starts crying. Paolo/Paola has a big heart. Let that heart show when Madrina cries.

PRE-K

Winter is talking to his/her mom while eating an after school snack and talking about the first days of school. Although Winter likes school, he/she really misses being at home with Mommy.

I don't want to go to school anymore. The first day was a lot of fun, but I don't want to go anymore. Yes, Miss Dina is very nice. But I miss you too much Mommy.

You are going to come tomorrow to class to read a book during story time? Really! Which one?

Okay, then tomorrow I will go, but then all the other days I am going to stay home with you and read our favorite books.

REHEARSAL DISCUSSION:

1. Why does Winter not want to go to school anymore?

2. What was your first day of Pre-K like? Do you remember how you felt when you first arrived?

3. What is the name of your teacher? Is she nice like Miss Dina?

4. What is Winter doing while he/she talks to mom?

5. How does Winter feel in the beginning of the monologue? How does Winter feel by the end?

DIRECTOR'S TIP:

Rehearse this monologue by experiencing the three
different feelings Winter experiences in the beginning,
middle and end of this piece. Write them down on your
script which is separated into 3 sections for you. I challenge
you to start the monologue experiencing how Winter feels
when he/she first comes home from school, and end the
monologue experiencing what he/she feels when he/she
realizes Mom is coming to school tomorrow. Try completely
opposite emotions! Rehearse the monologue a second time
by saying Winter's lines completely over the top. How does
this change the piece? Do you think it helps you feel what
Winter is feeling?

THE PINK DRESS

In this monologue, Kimmie is fighting with her mom about what to wear to their cousin's wedding.

I don't want to wear that ugly dress! Please Mom! Don't make me. I hate pink! Why do I have to dress like a princess when I want to be a soccer star?

Can I wear my new overalls to the wedding? Or my new Barcelona Soccer Jersey? Please Mom. They're more me than that ugly pink dress!

What does appropriate mean? I hate being appropriate! I just want to be allowed to be ME.

REHEARSAL DISCUSSION:

1. Have you ever fought with your mom about what clothes to wear? What did you want to wear and what did your mom want you to wear? How did you feel during this moment?

2. How would you describe Kimmie? What sport does she like to play? Do you think she likes the color pink?

3. What does the word "appropriate" mean?

4. What does Kimmie mean when she tells her mom, *"I just want to be allowed to be ME?"*

5. Where are Kimmie and her mom going?

DIRECTOR'S TIP:

Think of something you really don't like to wear. Be specific. Describe it in detail. Is it something itchy? What don't you like about it? Imagine you are wearing it right now. Experience it. Now, when you say your line, *"I don't want to wear that ugly dress,"* substitute it with your item and really experience what Kimmie is feeling. Give it a try.

THE LOLLIPOP

Andrew/Angelina wants a lollipop from Mom, but Mom won't give it to him/her

I want the lollipop Mom! Why can't I have it? A cavity! I don't care if I have a cavity. I still want my lollipop. GIVE IT TO ME!

I can have one after I go to the dentist? I am not going to the dentist. Last time I went, he put some weird things in my mouth and I was so scared. I don't want to go.

The dentist will give me a lollipop after the visit? Well since you won't give it to me, I guess I will have to get one from him. Let's go already! Come on. I want to make sure no one takes the red one!

REHEARSAL DISCUSSION:

1. What does Andrew/Angelina want in this monologue from Mom?

2. Why won't Mom give it to him/her?

3. What is a cavity? How do you get a cavity? Have you ever gotten one?

4. Do you like going to the dentist? Why or why not? How do you think Andrew/Angelina feels when Mom tells

him/her that they are going to the dentist today?

5. When Andrew/Angelina learns that the dentist will give him/her a lollipop, how does he/she react?

DIRECTOR'S TIP:

Write in Mom's lines anytime you think she says something. Then practice this monologue as if it was a scene between Mom and Andrew/Angelina. Pay attention to how you react to Mom when she says her lines and how Mom reacts to you when you say yours. Try your monologue again, this time really picturing your mom and hearing her lines. This will help you react authentically!

MISSING MATTHEW

Sadie is sad because her best friend Matthew has moved to a new state.

I don't want to play with anyone today. I want to be alone! I don't want to go swimming or go for ice cream. I miss Matthew. Matthew and I did everything together and now that he moved so far away my heart hurts. I don't want new friends. I want Matthew back. When I was cold, he would give me his jacket. And when I was scared to do something in the playground, Matthew would hold my hand. I have never done anything without Matthew.

He's calling me right now? Really! Give me the phone, quickly. *(Sadie talks on a phone)* Hey Matthew! You miss me? I really miss you too! Can we talk like this every day on the phone? Yay! How about we draw each other a picture, and then we can send it to one another! Okay, I'm going to go work on mine right now! Talk to you tomorrow. *(Sadie hangs up the phone.)* Mommy! Do you want to help me draw a picture for Matthew? He loves elephants! Let's draw a big elephant for him.

REHEARSAL DISCUSSION:

1. Why is Sadie so sad at the beginning of the monologue?

2. Have you ever had someone you were close to move away? How did that feel? If not, can you imagine if

your best friend moved and you could not see him/ her everyday? How would that make you feel? Can you imagine what Sadie is feeling?

3. Does Sadie use any props in this monologue? Which props does she use?

4. How many people is Sadie talking to during this monologue? Who are they?

5. How does Sadie's feelings change from the beginning to the end of the monologue? The script has been divided into 3 sections. Try writing in a different feeling for each section and act it out when you say your lines.

DIRECTOR'S TIP:

Sadie is talking to her Mom in this monologue, but then when Matthew calls, she is talking to him on the phone. We react differently according to who it is we are speaking to. Rehearse the monologue showing the switches from how Sadie is when she talks to Mom, compared to how she is when she talks to Matthew. Also, when she speaks to Matthew, she is on the phone. Rehearse using a phone as a prop, or simply mime it. Make sure you hear Matthew's voice on the other side of that phone. This will make your performance magical!

THE BABYSITTER'S BEDTIME

Mark/Mila does not want to go to bed, even though the babysitter says it's bedtime.

Please don't make me go to sleep yet. Mom never makes me sleep without giving me chocolate milk first. I know I already had popcorn, but she let's us drink chocolate milk too. I don't need a lot of rest, I'm a superhero. Superheroes don't need sleep at all. Besides, Mom and Dad won't care if I am up, as long as I am asleep by the time they get back from dinner.

Why are you yawning? Are you tired? Maybe you need some of my superpowers!

You know what? I think you are the one who needs to go bed. Here's my blanket. And don't worry, I'll wake you up when Mom and Dad come home. Good Night!

REHEARSAL DISCUSSION:

1. What does Mark/Mila want from the babysitter? Why?

2. Where and When does this monologue take place? Describe the setting in detail.

3. How does Mark/Mila feel about the babysitter?

4. Do you have a babysitter? What is it like when they babysit you?

5. Do you think Mom and Dad would be happy to know that Mark/Mila has not gone to bed yet? Why or why not?

DIRECTOR'S TIP:

Pay attention to the setting: Where and When this monologue takes place. What do you think Mark/Mila is wearing? Try rehearsing this monologue by creating the setting for bedtime. Take notice of how that changes your performance.

SNOW WHITE

Herason/Harry has always wanted a pet, but was never allowed to have one. Now that she/he has found Snow White, she/he wants to keep her.

Grammy, can we please keep the kitten I found? I already named her. I'm calling her Snow White because she is so white and pretty. She's also so soft and cold, just like the snow. She loves it when I rub her nose and play with her.

She needs me, so please can we keep her? But if you don't keep her, then I will never get to have a pet. I thought grandparents were supposed to give their grandchildren everything they wanted. Mom and Dad won't let me have a pet, so I thought you would. Gramps is allergic to cats? I didn't know that. Oh boy!

Grammy, I don't want to just put Snow White back outside all by herself. Sure, we can make signs to see if someone else wants to take her, but if they do, I hope they call her Snow White. She seems to like the name.

REHEARSAL DISCUSSION:

1. Why does Herason/Harry want their Grammy to keep Snow White?

2. Do you have a pet? If yes, describe how much your pet

means to you? If not, would you like a pet? Why?

3. Why does Grammy say "NO" when Herason/Harry asks her to keep the kitten? How does Herason/Harry feel when Grammy says, "No?"

4. How do you think Herason/Harry changes from the beginning of the monologue to the end?

5. Why did he/she name the kitten, "Snow White?"

DIRECTOR'S TIP:

Rehearse the scene pretending you have Snow White in your hands. Be consistent with her size and how you pet her. Really feel her soft fur. When you learn that Grammy will not let you keep her, how does this affect the way you continue to hold her?

TOYS

Devon does not want to give up his/her toys.

Do I have to give up those toys? I love that doll, so no, I am not giving her away. Wait, don't put my favorite drawing board in the box. So what if I don't use it? Maybe I will play with it tomorrow. Why are you making me throw away my toys? You are not nice!

Yes, I want other kids to play too, but why can't their mommy and daddy buy them their own toys so I can keep mine? Some kids don't have a mommy and daddy?! Why? That's not fair. All kids need a mom and dad. Who will take care of them when they get sick or feed them when they are hungry?

Mom, look at this lego set! We should add it to the box! I don't need all this stuff anymore. Maybe it will make another boy or girl smile the way it made me.

REHEARSAL DISCUSSION:

1. Have you ever had to give up toys that were yours? How did this make you feel?

2. What is your favorite toy? What is Devon's?

3. How does Devon feel when he/she learns that not every child has a mom and dad? Does this change how he/she feels about donating some of his/her toys?

4. Where does this scene take place?

5. What props do you imagine to be in this scene?

DIRECTOR'S TIP:

Rehearse this monologue by imagining where the scene takes place and all the many toys in this location. Is it in your playroom? Bedroom? Living room? Actually pantomime each toy you are using so that you can bring this monologue to life.

THE MIDDLE CHILD

Jimmy is tired of sharing with his brothers.

(Talking to his baby brother) No, you cannot have my elephant. It's mine! It's not yours. That's my horse. Hey, that's my rhino! Give it to me!

No Mama! I'm not letting him have my box of animals. Because they're mine! I don't care if I'm watching TV, he still can't play with them. I hate the baby. He tries to take all my toys.

Why did you give him my toys? It's not fair, I always have to share. I'm going to my room. No. I don't want you to hug me. I want you to give me my toys back. The baby always gets everything and Mario gets to have his own room. It's not fair. I'm tired of sharing everything with everyone!

REHEARSAL DISCUSSION

1. Are you the middle child in your family? If so, what is it like?

2. What is Jimmy feeling in this monologue?

3. Do you really think that Jimmy hates his baby brother? Why or why not?

4. Why did Jimmy's mother make him share his toys?

5. What are some of the advantages and disadvantages of being the middle child?

DIRECTOR'S TIP:

Jimmy is very emotional in this monologue. Discuss a time when you have experienced frustration and anger. Where do you feel those emotions in your body? Get your body moving before you do this monologue so that you have the physical energy to explode.

ENGAGED TO JAMESON

Theadora is so excited to announce to her parents that she has big plans to get engaged to Jameson, her older sister's friend.

Mommy! Daddy! I want Jameson to buy me a big diamond ring. He is so dreamy. He always smiles at me when we pick up Valentina from school. I want you to help me buy a pretty dress, because I'm going to ask him to propose to me on Christmas. Jameson will buy me the biggest diamond ring ever because he is so rich! What do mean you he's not rich? His daddy has a BMW!

Jameson likes Valentina? No he doesn't. He likes me. He always plays with me and ignores Valentina. I think you're wrong. He does not like her. You're just worried because you are too scared to have to pay for my wedding. I want a Cinderella wedding, and you guys better start saving because Jameson is going to be my Prince Charming. I will not let Valentina ruin my plans again. This time the younger sister will win!

REHEARSAL DISCUSSION:

1. How would you describe Theadora?

2. Who is Theadora talking to in this monologue? What does she want from them?

3. What is Theadora's obstacle?

4. How does Theadora feel about her older sister Valentina?

5. Do you think Jameson really likes Theadora? Why or why not?

DIRECTOR'S TIP:

This is a funny monologue, but don't play it for laughs. Commit to what Theadora is actually feeling and the humor will come out naturally.

Hollywood's Rising Stars Monologues

AGES 8-11

THE OLD LADY

Edwina/Edwin talks to Dad about the lonely old lady.

Dad, why does everyone make fun of that weird looking old lady who sits on the corner by herself? I know she wears dirty clothes and shakes a lot, but I don't know why people think it's funny. Jojo was making jokes about her and I pretended to laugh, but I really wanted to cry. She looks lonely Dad, and maybe if someone would talk to her they would know why she shakes and is always alone. I hope I am never alone like her. I sometimes think of what would I do if I was her. Do you think I can bring her this cookie you bought for me? Thanks Dad, I'll be right back.

REHEARSAL DISCUSSION:

1. Why does everyone make fun of the old lady?

2. Why does Edwina/Edwin pretend to laugh when Jojo makes jokes about the old lady?

3. Have you ever pretended to feel something even though inside you felt something else? Why did you hide your true feelings?

4. How do you think Edwina/Edwin changes from the beginning to the end of this monologue?

5. Have you ever felt lonely? Describe what it is like to feel that way.

DIRECTOR'S TIP:

Visualize the old lady. When you are sharing with your dad what she looks like and how people make fun of her, see her. This is the *movie rolling behind your eyes*. If the audience sees you visualizing it and it coming to life for you, it will come to life for them too.

THE PIANO LESSON

Gretchen/George wants to quit piano lessons.

Mom, I hate playing the piano. It's no fair. All the kids in our neighborhood get to ride bikes together after school, but I am stuck playing piano with dull Mrs. Kenny. Her breath smells and sometimes she falls asleep during our lesson. I know I used to love playing piano, but I love riding bikes too. Can I please quit Mom? Why are you going to give away my piano? No, don't do that! I love my piano. Maybe Mrs. Kenny can take a breath mint or two because I am not going to let you throw my piano away!

REHEARSAL DISCUSSION:

1. Do you play a musical instrument? Do you enjoy playing it? Why or why not?

2. Why does Gretchen/George want to quit piano lessons?

3. Why does the mom threaten to give away the piano? How does Gretchen/George react to that?

4. Do you think Gretchen/George likes playing the piano? Why or why not?

5. Can you relate to this monologue? How?

DIRECTOR'S TIP:

Why does Gretchen/George need to quit piano today?
Create a reason for why today is the day she/he must quit.
This will ground your monologue and make your objective-
wanting to quit, urgent! Try a few ideas out.

MY DRAWING OF NANNY

Alexandrea/Axel loves art and is serious about drawing. She/he painted a portrait of her/his grandmother and is very proud of it, until her/his parents explain that it might insult Nanny. This is hard for the young artist to understand.

Why can't I give this picture to Nanny? I worked so hard on it. Those are her wrinkles! Nanny has a lot of wrinkles, that's why I put them there. She'll love it. Do I want to hurt her feelings? No. I don't want to do that. But I think her wrinkles are pretty. That's why I took so long to make each one perfect. Of course I would never want to upset Nanny. How about if I make another picture without her wrinkles? Then will you let me give it to her? Okay, fine, but I will always prefer my first one. Why? Because it's real and beautiful, just like Nanny. I'll just keep it for me.

REHEARSAL DISCUSSION:

1. Write down 3 adjectives you would use to describe Alexandrea/Alex.

2. Why do his/her parents not want him/her to give the painting to Nanny?

3. What does Alexandrea/Alex mean when she/he says: *"I took time to make each wrinkle perfect?"*

4. How do you think Alexandrea/Alex feels during the monologue? Does it change throughout?

5. How do you think Alexandrea/Alex feels about Nanny? What do you call your grandmother? How do you feel about her?

DIRECTOR'S TIP:

Draw a picture of someone in your family. Take your time to make it perfect. This will help you empathize with Alexandrea/Alex.

SHOW AND TELL

Reza is upset because he has nothing to show to his class for Show and Tell today.

I am sorry class, but I don't have anything for my Show and Tell today because my brother broke it. He is a baby and my mom says he doesn't know any better. But I think he does. He always ruins everything of mine and now he ruined the model of the TITANIC I built. Sure, I can tell you how I built it Miss Joan, but I really wanted to show it to you. Little brothers ruin everything. Did I put my Titanic in a safe place? I put it on the floor. You think it's my fault that Jimmy broke it?! See, it's always my fault. Always! Little Brothers are pains!

REHEARSAL DISCUSSION:

1. What is Reza's problem in this monologue?

2. Have you ever built or made something that someone broke? How did this make you feel?

3. Do you think it is Jimmy's fault that Reza's Titanic broke? Why or why not?

4. How do you think Reza feels at the start of the monologue and how does that change by the end?

5. Do you agree with the line: *"Little Brothers are pains!"*

Why or why not? Do you think that Reza always feels this way?

DIRECTOR'S TIP:

Recall a time in your life that you could not be prepared for class because of something that happened. Write about it. Then, before you perform, read what you wrote and allow it to help you get into the character of Reza.

SORE LOSER

Vasili/Victoria is upset that his/her little cousin Alessia is beating him at the game they are playing.

Alessia, stop it. You are cheating! Yes you are. I am going to tell your mother if you don't stop. Jealous! Who me? I am not jealous of a 6 year old. I am not a sore loser! Stop singing that! If you throw that doll at me, you are going to pay for it little cousin! (*Vasili/Victoria chases Alessia around the room*) I will not let go of your hair until you say you are sorry. Say it. You hate me? Well… then I am really not going to let go! You think I am the worst cousin in the world? I am the only one who plays with you and puts up with your nonsense. Oh don't cry. I was only joking. All our other cousins love you too. I would never want another baby cousin besides you. Now let's just finish playing the game. You really got good at it!

REHEARSAL DISCUSSION:

1. What happened before the monologue begins? How will this determine how you are going to say your first line?

2. What game do you think they are playing? Pick one and then use it for your monologue.

3. Why do you think Vasili/Victoria called Alessia a

cheater? How do you think Alessia reacts to that comment?

4. What is Vasili/Victoria feeling when he/she is pulling Alessia's hair? Have you ever done something like this? Explain.

5. Have you ever been a sore loser when someone close to you started beating you during a game? How did losing make you feel?

DIRECTOR'S TIP:

Write in Alessia's lines and rehearse this as a scene. Grab a partner and actually act out playing all the actions. Then, rehearse it as monologue and take note of how the scene work helped you make this solo piece come to life.

THE CHOCOLATE CHIP COOKIE

Riven is trying to bribe her brother Billy into doing her homework.

Oh Billy! Look what I have here! A cookie! Your favorite kind! Yup, Mom's famous homemade chocolate chips! I would love to give you one, but it's the only one left, which means it's just for me. Unless, you will do something for me in return. I can only give you this delicious, warm, melt in your mouth chocolaty cookie, if you agree to do my homework for me so I can watch my favorite show. No, that would not be lying Billy! It's called doing business. An even exchange for services. That's right, I am a business woman now and that's how we roll! Fine, suit yourself. You can decline my offer, but I am going to eat this entire cookie all by myself. *(She eats the cookie and savors every bite.)* Yum. So good! And by the way, it stinks doing business with you Billy! *(She is ready to walk away, but then she turns around in desperation.)* Can you at least help me with my homework since you know how to do division? You would have helped me if I didn't eat the cookie! Oh boy!

REHEARSAL DISCUSSION:

1. What does Riven want from her brother Billy?

2. What obstacle does Riven face when trying to get what he/she wants?

3. Why does Riven want this from Billy?

4. How would you describe Riven? Write 3 sentences to describe her.

5. How does Riven change from the beginning to the end of the monologue?

DIRECTOR'S TIP:

Rehearse this with an actual chocolate chip cookie. How does using the prop enhance your performance?

THE PINK ROOM

Georgia is sick and tired of sharing a room with her little sister Sienna.
She confronts her mom regarding the issue.

Mom, you promised me a long time ago that once I started fourth grade I could have my own room. I hate sharing with Sienna. She snores and hops into bed with me every night with her smelly feet. And the room is baby blue. I want a pretty pink room with flowers all around like Madison's room. Her house is so much nicer than ours. Why do we have to live in this little apartment? It stinks here and the rooms are all so small! I don't care if people would die to live in this city. No, I'm not lucky. I'm unlucky and I'm sick and tired of not having privacy. If you want me to get good grades, I am going to need my own room. What? Did you just say what I think you said? You mean we can really paint our room pink? Flowers too? Well, I guess Sienna isn't so bad. I think I can manage putting up with her for a little while longer. Thanks Mom. *(as she runs off)* Hey, Sienna, want to sleep in my bed tonight?

REHEARSAL DISCUSSION:

1. What is happening in this monologue? What does Georgia want from her mother?

2. What is your favorite color? Is your bedroom that color? Why or why not?

3. Do you share your bedroom with your brother or sister?

4. In what city do you think Georgia lives? Why do cities have small apartments?

5. Does Georgia get what she wants at the end? Why or why not?

DIRECTOR'S TIP:

How will you end the monologue? Rehearse it by running off and calling Sienna at the end.

THE VALENTINE

Abby writes her own Valentine Card to herself, but signs it from her school crush Juan.

What is this? A Valentine for me! I wonder who could have sent this to me. I didn't know I had an admirer. Should I open it now or wait till I get home? Okay, okay, I'll open it. *(She opens the Valentine Card and begins to read)* "Dear Abigail, you are the love of my life. Ever since we met in first grade at The Little Red School House and had to stand on line together I knew you were the one. Every day in class I looked at you hoping that one day you would notice me too. Abigail Brown, will you be mine? Love always, Juan." Jessica, isn't he the sweetest thing? I had no idea that my crush felt like this too. I'm so so so so so happy. Wait! Where are you going? No, don't ask him if he sent this to me! Of course he did! Why would I make that up? Do you think I'm actually crazy enough to write this to myself? *(Jessica grabs Juan and brings him over to Abby.)* Hey, Juan! Right you wrote me this Valentine? *(She looks at him with puppy dog eyes begging him to say yes.)* Huh? That's strange. Well then if you didn't write it, who did? Maybe there is another Juan in the class and we didn't know it! Oh wait! I get it! You're too embarrassed to admit that you love me. Don't worry Juan! I promise not to tell anyone about our little secret. P.S. I love you too!

REHEARSAL DISCUSSION:

1. Have you ever had a crush on someone from school? Who? How does your crush make you feel?

2. Who does Abby have a crush on? What is his name?

3. What does Abby want from Jessica when she is reading the Valentine from "Juan?" Why does she want this?

4. Does Abby get what she wants from Jessica? Why or Why not?

5. What does Abby do when Juan comes over? How do you think she feels?

DIRECTOR'S TIP:

Create a Valentine's Day Card to read during the monologue. This will make your performance more real.

AMERICAN GIRL DOLL

Mikayla has saved $20 from doing chores. The problem is she still needs $80 more to buy the American Girl Doll that she wants. Her parents think the price of the doll is ridiculous and said Mikayla will have to wait for a special occasion if she wants one. Mikayla does not want to wait, so she comes up with a little plan.

Mikayla: *(looking in a mirror and counting her teeth, as her sister Sadie walks in)* 1-2-3-4-5-6-7-8-9-...Oh hey Sadie. I'm just counting my teeth. I might need you to help me pull some out, okay? Because I need to make money. Every time the tooth fairy comes she has left me $5. So far I have saved $20, but I need eighty more dollars to buy my American Girl Doll. Mom and dad won't buy it for me, so I figured if can lose 16 teeth, I'll make the money and buy one for myself. I don't need anyone to give me the money anyway. I'm independent. You know what Sadie, you should start taking some notes from your big sister so you can learn how to be successful in life too. What? What do you mean I'm acting ridiculous? This is a genius idea and you know it! You're too young to know about making money anyway! *(She looks back in the mirror and tries to start pulling out some teeth.)* So are you just going to stand there, or are you going to help me pull out some teeth? My smile? What about it? Hmmm... I didn't think about that. That's true, I didn't think about chewing either. Well, maybe I just won't smile or chew for a while! I just really want an American Girl Doll!

REHEARSAL DISCUSSION:

1. Do you have an American Girl Doll? Which one?

2. What is Mikayla doing at the start of the monologue? How do you think her sister Sadie reacts to this when she first walks in and sees her staring in the mirror counting her teeth?

3. How would you describe Mikayla? Write down 3 adjectives to describe her in this scene and then try incorporating them into your performance.

4. Have you ever pulled out your own tooth? If yes, how did it feel?

5. Have you ever wanted something as badly as Mikayla wants an American Girl doll? What was it? Why did you want it? Did you ever get it?

DIRECTOR'S TIP:

When you are rehearsing this monologue, actually count your teeth in front of a real mirror so that you can remember what you did. Then, recreate it when it is time to perform.

ALL I WANT FOR CHRISTMAS

Unlike all of her friends, Veronica/Vince does not want toys for Christmas. There is only one thing she/he wants and she/he is hoping Santa can help.

Veronica/Vince: (writing a letter) Dear Santa, I hope you will be the person to actually read this. When I go to Macy's every year to meet you, I noticed that you look very different from the Santa in The Radio City Christmas Spectacular. Then, when I walk on the streets, sometimes I see one of you at every corner, and you are all dressed the same, but look different. I asked my aunt once why there were so many of you, and she explained to me that you are so busy up in The North Pole that you have to send your helpers out to help you. You even have them dress like you. Since my aunt never lies to me, I believe her. However, I am writing to you hoping that you are the one to read this letter and not one of your helpers, as it is really important Santa. Every year for Christmas you have brought me a lot of toys and I've loved them. My Mom always told me that it was because I was so good all year. Well this year I have been extra good because I want one very special gift. Santa, all I want for Christmas is for you to get my mom and dad back together again. When Daddy moved out, Mom changed. She's always so upset and I see her crying by herself a lot. I hate seeing her so unhappy. I also miss seeing my dad every morning. When he left, he never came back to our home. Please Santa! I know if someone can bring my parents back together again, it's you. Thank you! And don't worry, I won't tell the other kids that the Radio City Santa is just an actor. It will be our little secret! Love, *Veronica/Vince*

REHEARSAL DISCUSSION:

1. What is *Veronica/Vince* doing during this monologue? Who is she talking to?

2. What does *Veronica/Vince* want from Santa and why does she/he want it?

3. What is The Radio City Christmas Spectacular? If you don't know it, google it and read about this performance so that you can understand what *Veronica/Vince* means when she/he mentions it.

4. Have you ever met Santa in person? What is he like? Have you ever asked him for a special gift like *Veronica/Vince*? What did you ask for?

5. How would you describe what *Veronica/Vince* is feeling in this monologue? Have you ever felt something similar?

DIRECTOR'S TIP:

Once you have memorized this piece 110%, practice this monologue while actually writing the letter. Allow yourself to feel *Veronica/Vince* words as you write.

DOGS GO TO HEAVEN TOO

Arabella/Angelo comes home from school and is shocked to not be greeted by her/his dog Cupcake. When Arabella/Angelo looks for Cupcake and calls her name, she/he realizes that she is not there. She/ he then finds her Dad and asks him to tell her/him where Cupcake is.

Cupcake! Cupcake! Where are you? Time to go to the park and play! I have your favorite ball. Cupcake! Where did you go? *(panicked)* DAD! DAD! Where's Cupcake? I cannot find her anywhere. What do you mean you took her to the doctor? Is she sick? Can you bring me there so that I can go see her? She hates the doctor and she would want me there with her. She's sleeping there? Let's just wake her up then and bring her home. I have so many things to tell her today. I need to tell her how Jack is still making fun of me. Every time Jack does that, Cupcake licks me and I feel better. I need to wake her up. I don't understand Dad! What do you mean the doctor put her to sleep? Was she tired? You mean she will never wake up again? Heaven! Why did she go to heaven? I want her to come home! I need her Dad. She loves me. Please let me try to wake her up. Maybe she just needs to see me. She can't go to heaven. She just can't. I need my best friend. *(hysterical)* Cupcake! If you hear me, come back! I love you so much!

REHEARSAL DISCUSSION:

1. Who is Cupcake? How would you describe the relationship between Arabella/Angelo and Cupcake?

2. Why do you think Arabella/Angelo panics when she/he cannot find Cupcake? Have you ever panicked when you could not find someone you loved? Recall the experience. Describe it in detail.

3. Why does Arabella/Angelo want to tell Cupcake about Jack making fun of her/him? Who do you think Jack is? How do you think he is making fun of Arabella/Angelo? How do you think this makes her/him feel?

4. What does Dad mean when he says: *"The doctor put Cupcake to sleep?"*

5. How do you think Arabella/Angelo feels by the end of this monologue? Have you ever felt this way? If not, can you imagine feeling this way? What in your life would make you feel this?

DIRECTOR'S TIP:

This is an emotional scene. Before you perform this monologue, allow yourself some time to emotionally prepare. Use the questions below to bring you into the world of Arabella/Angelo. If you have a beloved pet, imagine what it would be like to lose him or her. Allow yourself to experience a wave of emotions. When you can relate to the given circumstances above, you will then be ready to perform this piece.

Hollywood's Rising Stars Monologues

AGES 12-15

THE CELL PHONE

Sing/Soh really wants a cell phone and in this scene she/he is convincing her/his mom to buy her/him one.

I can't believe that it's my birthday and you still won't get me what I want. I don't want to go on a vacation or see another Broadway play. Yes, of course I enjoy doing that, but what's the point if I can't share it on Instagram or Snap Chat. Everyone of my friends has a phone but me, and now that I'm 12, almost a teen, I think that I am old enough to have a phone. No one can survive without one, so it's weird that you think I can. I don't care if you did not get a phone until you were an adult. Besides, phones didn't even exist then because times are different Mom. We are no longer in the Stone Ages! You are the strictest Mom of all my friends and one day you are going to have to trust me. What about if I am in an emergency situation? Or imagine I get sick and I need to call 911! I will have no way to call for help!

What did you say? Ummmm….Yes, of course I promise to only use it during designated hours and never at the table! You really will get me a phone? Oh Mom, this is the best birthday ever.

No, of course I won't accept your request on TikTok? I live with you, so why do you need to follow me? What? You want to limit the amount of calls and texts I can make and receive? This is crazy. Oh great…and you want to see everywhere I am at every single moment! Are you a stalker Mom? I knew there was a catch!

REHEARSAL DISCUSSION:

1. Do you have a cell phone? How old were you when you got one? Were you parents willing to get you a phone, or are they still not ready?

2. Why do you think Sing/Soh wants a phone so badly?

3. Do you agree with the line, *"No one can survive without one, so it's weird that you think I can?"* If so, why? If not, why not?

4. What does Sing/Soh mean when she/he says, *"We are no longer in the Stone Ages?"*

5. Does Sing/Soh get what she/he wants from Mom? How do you know this? At what point of the monologue? Why do you think Mom gave in? Make sure to mark this on your script.

DIRECTOR'S TIP:

Pay attention to Mom in this monologue, even though her lines are not written into the script. Sing/Soh has to react to Mom. When Mom finally agrees to give Sing/Soh the cell phone, really take it in and show us how happy you are to have gotten what you wanted.

LIKE LIKE LIKE LIKE YOU!

Marina is trying hard to be nice when rejecting Jake's offer to go out.

Look, you're really nice Jake, but it's my first day of school here and I want to get a head start on my homework. But thank you for the invite. Maybe I'll join you guys some other time. Yes, I'm sure. Oh no, I don't need you to help me with my homework, but thank you for the offer. Tomorrow? Well, I can't tomorrow. Friday? No that doesn't work either. I don't know how to say this without offending you, but I'll try. I like you, but I don't *like like* you. Meaning I like you as a friend, not as a boyfriend. Oh, you weren't asking me out? You totally were. You don't *like like* me either. Well, why not? I'm a catch! You know what, just because you said that, I will go out with you on Friday and and you will fall for me, like in a way where you *like like like like* me! How dare you say you just see me as a friend! That was so rude!

REHEARSAL DISCUSSION:

1. Why does Marina initially turn down Jake's invite?

2. What does Marina mean when she says, "I don't *like like* you?"

3. Have you ever told anyone that you don't *like like* them? Was it difficult to say? Explain.

4. Why does Marina react so confused when she discovers Jake was not asking her out? What do you think about her reaction?

5. Do you think Jake really sees Marina as just a friend? Why or why not?

DIRECTOR'S TIP:

Really switch emotionally when Marina discovers Jake only likes her as a friend. There is humor in that and it's all in the timing. Have fun rehearsing and try different choices until you find the strongest one.

WILL YOU BE MY SISTER?

Donna is sleeping over at her best friend Suzie's house. Suzie's younger siblings are bothering the girls and want to hang out with them. Suzie is annoyed, as she just wants to be with Donna. In this monologue: Donna talks to Suzie about how lucky she is to have siblings, even though they annoy her.

Suzie, don't worry about Fiona coming into your room. I really don't mind. Really, I don't. I kind of like all the chaos when I come to your house. I know she annoys you, but maybe if you don't react she'll stop bothering us eventually. Honestly, you're so lucky to have a little sister and brother. It gets lonely being an only child.

Do you want to know what the absolute worst part about being an only child is? Having no one to share the hard times with. My parents are getting a divorce! They told me last week and they tried to make it look like a fun new experience. They're such bad actors because they were both forcing smiles on their faces and trying to get me all excited about having two bedrooms now. They were pretending that it will be a great thing that I'll get to spend every other weekend with my dad. My father made sure I knew that we'll go away together and do things we'd never do before. And as I sat there and watched my parents try to convince me that my life would be better, I was wishing that I had a sister or brother to cry with, to sleep with that night. Someone else who'd understand how awful it is to learn that your parents will no longer be husband and wife. But, instead, I went to my room and laid in my dark, cold bedroom staring at the ceiling all by myself the whole night. I couldn't go to sleep. I felt so alone.

That's why you're lucky to have siblings. During the hard times, you'll have people that will also be going through it with you. *(Suzie asks Donna to be her sister and Donna is touched.)* You're so sweet, I would love to be your sister, but you already have Fiona as your sister. You want two sisters? Come on…Really! Are you sure? Wow! Thank you, Suzie. This is the best offer someone has ever made me. Now can we please watch a movie, and make a tent with Fiona and Tommy. Let's pretend we are all one big crazy family tonight, okay?

REHEARSAL DISCUSSION:

1. Why does Donna think Suzie is lucky to have siblings?

2. Are you an only child? If not, do you know anyone who is an only child? What differences are there between an only child and a family with siblings? Write them down.

3. How do you think Donna feels about her parents getting a divorce? Do you know anyone whose parents are divorced? How did the divorce affect them?

4. How do you think Suzie reacts to Donna's news about the divorce?

5. Describe the character of Donna using 3 adjectives.

DIRECTOR'S TIP:

Circle the little moments in the script. A look, a smile, an uncomfortable silence, a frown. Sometimes the moments between the lines are just as important. Don't be afraid of pauses. You can say so much about a character's experiences with one look, one eye roll, one motivated pause. During your rehearsal, be sure to capture these little moments.

I AM NOT NEUROTIC, I'M SMART!

Angelina is a 12 year old girl who loves dogs more than people. In this monologue, Angelina is seen talking to her vet. She wants her vet to confirm that she is not NEUROTIC!

Dr. DiPaolo, thank you so much for examining Ginger again. I know you said you would call to give me the results of her lyme disease test, but I figured what the heck, I might as well stop by and find out in person. I know this might sound weird to you Doc, but I love coming here. I really do. My parents get angry that I come so much. They said Ginger's vet bills are more expensive than my entire family's medical bills for the year, but you know, Ginger is getting older and well it's important for me to maintain her health, don't you think? See, you get me, unlike my family. My annoying cousin Dave was teasing me the whole time on our family camping trip and he kept calling me neurotic. I really don't like him. I don't think I'm neurotic Doc, I just think I'm smarter and more prepared than everyone else and can sense dangerous situations more so than others. Dave thought I was ridiculous for bringing 10 bottles of DEET with me. I come prepared.

According to Dave, DEET is poisonous and so he convinced my whole family to not use any harmful chemicals. My Aunt Josie was completely on his side. She said, *"Angelina, can't we all just live a little and enjoy some nature?"* And then, Dave dared me in front of my whole family. He dared me to leave Ginger behind with our Uncle Ted so that I could join the rest of our family for a long hike and swim. I didn't want to. I don't trust Uncle Ted. Heck, I don't trust anyone with Ginger other than you Doc. But Dave was so persistent and annoying, and so, I gave in. Of course, once we returned from our hike, I was right. I should have never left Ginger with irresponsible Uncle Ted! I found Uncle Ted sleeping, like snoring kind of sleep, not watching Ginger at all. Who does that? Who falls asleep when they are supposed to be responsible for watching over a living thing? GINGER WAS ROLLING AROUND IN DEER POOP! Yes, quite disgusting! Even my mother was upset. She too knew this meant only one thing. TICKS! Yup, Ginger was full of ticks, and well they must of all jumped onto the rest of my family because we spent the rest of our vacation picking ticks off of one another. See! I should have never listened to obnoxious Dave. We needed to be wearing DEET after all. It's common sense.

What did the nurse just give to you? Oh my, are those Ginger's results? I'm so worried. If she has lyme I'm going to call up my awful cousin Dave and give him a piece of my…what?! Did you just say NEGATIVE? Are you sure? How accurate is the test? Oh Ginger, did you hear that, you are going to be okay. You're absolutely fine my baby girl! Oh Dr. DiPaolo, thank you. Thank you so much. I will come in next month for a re-check, just in case the test is flawed. See, a neurotic person would want a retest now, like right this second, but I am willing to wait a month. Thanks Doc. Bye. *(She is about to leave, but suddenly stops)* Oh my God, Ginger just sneezed. Doc, Wait! Is that normal? I mean she never sneezes. I heard sneezing can be the sign of something really serious. Dr. DiPaolo, can you check her just one last time?

REHEARSAL DISCUSSION:

1. Investigate- Write down all the facts in the script.

2. Inference- Next to each fact, write your opinion. For instance, one fact is: Angelina goes to the vet often with her dog Ginger. What does this say about Angelina? Write this down for each fact you find.

3. Invention- Once you completed questions 1 & 2- now you can start making choices. How do you think Angelina should be played? What conclusions have you made about her?

4. Ginger: You have a dog in your monologue. How will you convey this to the audience? Will you pet an imaginary dog? Will you use a stuffed animal? The possibilities are endless.

5. How would you definite a neurotic person? Do you think Angelina is neurotic? Why or why not? Can you relate to her in areas of your life? Write them down.

DIRECTOR'S TIP

Have fun reaching the emotional heights in this monologue. How does Angelina's emotions shift through the course of the monologue?

MEAN GIRLS

Amalia, a 14 year old student is having trouble with some friends at school. She is torn between her childhood friend Dina and the popular girl Kelly. She wants to be a part of Kelly's cool group, but that means she will have to give up her friendship with Dina. This has been causing problems for her at school. In this monologue, Amalia is talking to her mother Leila. She is trying to convince Leila to let her be homeschooled, as she cannot bear another day being around the Mean Girls!

Mom, close my door. I don't feel good, that's why. There's no way I can go to school today. I think I have a fever. Please just leave me alone, I need to rest. Nothing is wrong! And if you really were concerned about me, you would never make me go to school again. I want to be homeschooled from now on. Okay?

(Amalia breaks down into tears, but fights to hide it from her mother.) Please just get out and leave me alone. Kelly had a sleep over this weekend and she did not invite me. Okay?! Happy now? I found out on SnapChat. She was posting photos all night. How could she not invite me after all we've done this past month together? I thought we were friends. Mom, my life is so messed up. I want to fit in so badly with Kelly and those girls, but that means I cannot be friends with Dina. They think Dina is strange, which you have to admit, she is a little. And anytime they see me with her, they don't want to be around me. I have tried to pull away from Dina as

much as possible. Dina and I have been friends forever and I love her, I do, but I also want to make new friends. And Kelly, well, she's cool Mom. I feel important when I'm with her and her group. I don't feel invisible the way I do when I'm with Dina.

The other day at lunch, I was sitting with Kelly and all the other popular kids. It was so much fun! But then I saw Dina sitting all by herself. I felt so bad seeing her all alone, and so I sat down next to her so she could have someone to eat her lunch with. One hour later, I see Kelly making mean comments underneath my Instagram photos saying that I am not a loyal friend. She then ignored me in science class and everyone else followed her. No one would talk to me. I don't understand why I can't just be friends with everyone. Do you see why I don't want to go to school now? I think I liked it better when I was invisible. It was easier than reading mean comments about myself and being purposely ignored.

Dina is my true friend. I guess I just wanted to know what it was like to be cool and popular. Turns out, it's overrated. Mom, I would love to continue talking, but I better get ready for school. Dina is going to need her lunch buddy. I'll be ready in ten. And Mom…thank you. It's really nice talking with you. Let's do it more often.

REHEARSAL DISCUSSION:

1. Why was Amalia pretending to be sick in the beginning of the monologue?

2. Have you ever pretended to be sick so that you did not have to go to school? How did that work out for you? Why did you do it?

3. How would you describe Kelly? Would you want to be friends with someone like her? Do you have someone in your school who is similar to Kelly? Who? Describe her.

4. How would you describe Dina? Why do you think she sits alone at lunch? Do you know anyone in your school who sits alone at lunch too? How does that make you feel?

5. How would you describe Amalia's relationship to her mom? She almost did not share with her mom what was wrong with her. Do you share everything with your mom? Why or why not?

DIRECTOR'S TIP:

MASKING: In the beginning of this monologue, Amalia is wearing a mask. She is hiding from her mom what she is really feeling. She then removes her mask and allows her mom to see her inner feelings. Where on the script does this happen? Mark it. What motivates it? After she reveals her problem, she goes even a little deeper. When do we learn Amalia's truest feelings? Allow yourself to show all the emotional layers of Amalia in this piece.

NOT READY TO SAY GOODBYE

Koda/Kylie is trying to convince his/her mother to not put Grandma into a nursing home. This is an emotional piece. Make sure you do all the work to connect to this piece.

Mom, I don't understand. Why can't Grandma just stay here? Why are you bringing her to a nursing home? She doesn't belong there. I can't believe you are doing this Mom. I'll never forgive you. Ever! If it's the best thing for Grams than tell me why she was crying yesterday all by herself? So what if Grams is not like the way she used to be? I don't care if she forgets to leave the stove on. I can turn it off. You have to be more patient with her Mom. Of course I want Grams to be safe. But I think we can help her be safe here. I can help you Mom. I can quit school and be homeschooled instead. Please Mom. I know she is not the same Grams anymore. I know.

I want Grams to be the way she used to be so badly. She always had more energy than everyone, and no one cooks Thanksgiving dinner like her, not even you. I miss that and I feel so sad inside that she is no longer the way she used to be. I keep praying that one day she will be the Grams I know. Sometimes she doesn't even remember who I am. When that happens, I hold her hand in mine! Once she feels me, I know she knows I am someone she loves, and that's all that matters. I don't want Grams to get hurt. I guess I am just not ready to say goodbye and lose hope that maybe her memory will come back one day.

Mom, I want to come with you to bring Grams to her new home, so don't leave without me, okay? And we can visit her everyday like you said, right? Even if she doesn't know we are there, we will!

REHEARSAL DISCUSSION:

1. What is this monologue about? In as few words as possible, articulate what happens.. Once you understand what is happening, you can begin to examine the many ways to play it out.

2. What happened right before the monologue begins?

3. What do you want from the person whom you are speaking to?

4. Why do you want it?

5. What will you lose if you don't get it?

DIRECTOR'S TIP:

Playing emotional scenes can be challenging and we don't want to fake the emotions, but rather connect to them. To start working on an emotional piece, it is highly advisable to begin with relaxation exercises to physically open up your body and mind. If your body is tense, it will get in the way of freeing your emotions. So, relax your head and roll your neck around. Breathe deeply through you nose and exhale out your mouth.

Once you do this, you can start preparing. First, identify the feelings your character is experiencing. Next, connect with these emotions by asking your yourself: *How would I feel if this was happening to me?* Or, perhaps you have had a similar situation in the past that can help you connect to what your character is experiencing. If so, try using it to connect to this monologue.

HOMEWORK IS A WASTE OF TIME

Ryder is talking to his acting coach.

How am I feeling? I'm tired. It's been a long day. First, I had to wake up for school and I didn't want to because I was up all night playing video games. I almost won this one game I've been trying to win for months, but then my mom came in my room and unplugged it. That was not cool of her. She thinks I need rest for school, but she doesn't understand, school just makes me tired. I do most of my sleeping in class.

Yeah, I heard what you asked. You asked, "Why didn't I do my acting homework?" What was it again? Oh yeah, to memorize my dramatic monologue. To be honest with you, I really don't like working on dramatic pieces. Playing other characters as it is just feels weird to me. I remember the first time I did a monologue in front of a group of people, it freaked me out. I was supposed to be somebody else, but I was still me, yet I wasn't, and I don't know…it's just weird you know. But as far as my acting homework goes, I honestly forgot. Truth. Yes, that's what every teacher says. You have to do your homework in order to grow. But it makes no sense. Kids go to school and learn all day. If they don't get their work done in class, then they should have to do homework. But that's it. Otherwise, it is just a waste of time and it causes us kids to fight with our parents and get video games taken away from us. It's not fair. Homework should not exist.

True, I guess acting homework is slightly different because I do need to memorize my lines in order to perform. Can you send me the monologue again? This time I will try not to lose it. Great. So next week we can work on my monologue, but for this week can we just do those great relaxation exercises you do where you have me lie on the floor with my eyes closed and talk to me in a soothing voice. Those really help me grow as a performer. You are the best acting coach! I wish all my teachers were like you!

REHEARSAL DISCUSSION

1. Do you agree with Ryder and the title of this monologue: "Homework is a waste of time"? Why or why not?

2. Who is Ryder? How would you describe him? Be specific. Write down three adjectives.

3. How do you think Ryder stands, walks, sits and moves? Every move, gesture, facial expression must come from your character.

4. What does Ryder want from his acting coach and why does he want it?

5. How do you think Ryder's acting coach is reacting to him? What makes you think this?

DIRECTOR'S TIP:

Tactics/Actions- Question #4 above asks: What does Ryder want from his Acting Coach? Write down 10 tactics/action choices Ryder can take to get what he wants. For example: To complain, To criticize, To whine. Then try using different actions any time there is a shift in the monologue. This will give your performance life!

YOU CAN'T QUIT!

Bam is seen sitting on a bench in the school playground crying. Belle sees her younger step sister and walks over to her immediately to comfort her.

You quit? You can't quit! You're Annie and the show is two weeks away! You know what this is? Last minute nerves. The same thing used to happen to me before a big gymnastic competition. It still does. It's normal. Come on, I will walk you back to the auditorium.

What's gotten into you? All you've done this whole year is talk about how badly you wanted the part of Annie, and now that it's yours, you want to quit? I don't get it. Diana and Lisa have been making fun of how you sing? Really? Do you think that I'm going to let you just quit like this, after I've had to listen to you sing every song from the show all day long for a year… because of Diana and Lisa? Come on! Get up! They cast you. You're going to be amazing!

You know I would never lie to you, right? So listen to me. As someone who is older than you, I can assure you that Diana and Lisa are just jealous of you. That's why they said those mean things to you. You are talented, you hear me. You can't let their words affect you like this. You are meant to be Annie! What do you say we walk back to school and go into that rehearsal together?

REHEARSAL DISCUSSION

1. How would you describe the relationship between Belle and Bam?

2. Why did Bam leave rehearsal?

3. Have you ever been in a situation similar to Bam? What happened? Describe it in detail.

4. Do you think Belle is a good older step sister? Why or why not?

5. Have you ever had to encourage someone in your life who was feeling down and defeated? Who was it? What did you say? How did you feel?

DIRECTOR'S TIP:

Listen to Bam's words even though she is not there. Belle is affected by Bam's pain, and therefore everything she says is a reaction to Bam. Try writing Bam's lines down and play this as a scene to practice.

AGES 12–15

THE MONNORS

Connor is so in love with Mary that he has even combined their names.
Connor + Mary = Monnor!

If I tell you Mom then you have to promise not to tell all your friends, especially Dad! Dad just won't understand young love. Promise with all your heart! Okay…so there's this girl in my class. Her name is Mary and I am in love with her. She loves me too. She told me the other day. But then on Monday, I saw her talking to Jake and it bothered me. I was angry at her. I was so upset I almost cried, but I didn't because boys are not supposed to cry, or at least that is what Dad told me. She apologized, but then she told me that she will still talk to other boys because she can love me and have other friends at the same time. It's hard for me to see that, but I am going to keep cool. I don't want her to think I'm some jealous dork or something. Anyway, the only reason why I'm telling you this is because our birthdays are one week a part and we want to do a combined birthday party. We want to call it **THE MONNORS!** Who are the Monnors? We are! When you combine our names, Connor and Mary, it is Monnor. What do you mean I'm too young to have a girlfriend? I'm 12 years old! I'm in love! Haven't you ever been in love before? Wait! Don't answer that. Besides, if we throw a party together, I won't have to worry about all her other "boyfriends" wanting to talk to her.

89

They will all know that they are only there to celebrate us Monnors. What do you say Mom?

REHEARSAL DISCUSSION

1. Do you think Connor is really in love with Mary? Why or why not?

2. Why does Connor not want his mother to tell anyone that he is in love with Mary?

3. How would you describe Connor?

4. What does Connor want from his mother? Does he get it?

5. Why does Connor want it?

DIRECTOR'S TIP:

Have you ever had a crush on someone before? Think about that person as you talk about Mary in this monologue. Explore all the feelings you experience when you have a crush.

WORRIED ABOUT MOM

Jake confronts his Grandmother about his Mom's drinking problem.

Grammy, I'm worried about Mom. Have you noticed that she always looks so sad all the time? She has not slept in the same room with Dad for over a year, and when he's around she looks even more miserable. She drinks wine every night. I know wine is not bad for you Grammy, but Mom does not drink just one glass. From the moment we come home from school, she is drinking and sometimes can go through 2 bottles a night. The other night she came home and asked me if she paid the babysitter. She forgot, and she didn't even pay the sitter. She was too drunk! I paid her for Mom. I have to always be on such high alert to make sure things are done because Mom is not capable anymore. She even forgets to feed the dog. I'm scared Grammy. Do you think Mom will ever stop drinking?

REHEARSAL DISCUSSION

1. Do you think Jake's grandmother is also concerned about Jake's Mom? Why or why not?

2. Why is Jake opening up to his grandmother about his Mom's drinking issue?

3. What is alcoholism? What is it like to live with an alcoholic?

4. How would you describe Jake?

5. What do you think Jake wants from his grandmother?

DIRECTOR'S TIP:

Research what it's like for children living with parents who have drinking problems. Use your research to develop your character.

Hollywood's Rising Stars Monologues

AGES 16-18

THE DIARY

Meg is talking to her teacher.

Thank you Miss Grey for seeing me during your lunch break. I wanted to come in to tell you that I did something kind of bad yesterday... okay pretty bad! But, I also learned a lot from what I did and I think it has helped me to find some compassion for my mother. Which is a great step for me, right? I mean last week when we spoke I told you how much I hated her.

As you know I am struggling with Lisa's eating disorder. My whole family is. I also feel responsible because, well you know, she is my twin sister and I can't help her. I always thought maybe if we had a normal mom, a kind one, this would've never happened to Lisa. Like maybe right now she wouldn't be in a rehab facility, all 98 pounds of her. She is all by herself there without me and it stinks. This is the first time we have ever been separated and it's taken a bit to get used to. Ever since I could remember our mom was constantly on us about our weight. She is the reason why I have such a toxic relationship with food. There are days where I eat everything to get revenge on her, and than other times when I eat nothing. Yes, I mean nothing at all because I am afraid she'll think I'm fat. I want to avoid hearing her criticize me, so I just starve. But I've never gone off the edge like my sister has, where I have needed to be hospitalized.

For some reason, I always find the strength to gain balance again.

What did I do that was so bad? Okay, well yesterday when my mom went on her daily bike ride with her fitness group, I went into her bedroom and I read her diary. Her entire diary from front to back! I cried the whole time while I read it. I thought my mom would be criticizing me and my sister throughout, but instead she praised us. But she criticized herself. Every single day, on every little page, my mom records her weight and keeps a log of everything she ate and every bit of exercise she has done. She is never satisfied and is hard on herself, every day. You see, my mom is struggling with an eating disorder too. Even though she is the most in shape person I know, she sees herself as someone who is fat and not good enough. Reading this made me stop hating her for a second. It made me want to hug her, and ever since I became a teenager, I have not hugged my mom. Not even once. Now I have two people in my life to help, my mom and my sister, and it's a lot Miss Grey. But I came here to tell you that I've got it all under control. I have to. If I don't, then who does?

Thank you for always listening. Our talks always help me so much!

REHEARSAL DISCUSSION

1. How would you describe the relationship between Meg and Ms. Grey?

2. Who is Meg? Answer as many details about your character as you can including: name, age, address, family, interests, dislikes, hobbies, physical traits, etc.

3. What does Meg want from Ms. Grey? Why does she want it?

4. What does Meg do to get what she wants?

5. How is the monologue structured: What is the Beginning, Middle and End? If you had to title each section, what would they be called?

DIRECTOR'S TIP:

Research Eating Disorders. Find out what it is like to have one. Discover what it is like to live with a family member who has one. How can you apply your research to playing the role of Meg?

YOUTUBE STAR!

Amy is talking to her parents about quitting school to become a YouTube star. She wants them to support her decision, but they are not at all happy about this idea!

Mom! Dad! Calm down. No need to get yourselves all crazy. You are making it sound like me not going to college is the worst thing in the world. My whole life I did everything exactly the way you wanted me to. I have gotten straight A's every year, won piano competitions, was the president of the student council for 2 consecutive years and I was the star of my track team. I have proved that I'm a good student and I don't see why going to college will help me with my current career goals. Being a YOUTUBE STAR is a career! You guys just don't understand the importance of my new Vlog. I thought you would be happy to learn that I am not leaving you to go away to some fancy school, and that you guys don't have to be Empty Nesters just yet. But, apparently you want me OUT of your way! Don't worry, as soon as I get my first million followers, I will pack up and leave. No, I am not being irrational. You can make more money on YouTube than you can make from any stupid job you get when you graduate college. How? By being ready for any opportunity: brands, shows, books, appearances — the list goes on. The opportunities are endless.

That's a great question Dad. I am happy you asked! My youtube show is going to be all about me and my life! I will be vlogging about what I eat for breakfast, to what toothpaste I brush my teeth with, the coffee I order, the reality television shows I am obsessed with... life. That was rude Mom! If you think my life is not all that interesting then you two are to blame for it. You gave me the perfect life. It's not my fault I have no drama and you think I am boring. Why are you two fighting now? Stop screaming! Actually, this is good stuff. Keep at it! *(She begins to take a video of them from her iPhone.)* Mom can you just move to your right a little bit, and Dad that was great. Say that to mom exactly the way you just did it before, and do not eliminate the cursing. Yes, of course I'm filming your fight. It's brilliant! This scene will be on my first video, my big debut. Continue yelling at each other! This is exactly the kind of stuff my audience will want to see.

Wait! Maybe you guys are right. Maybe I am boring! No one wants to see my parents fighting. Okay, you win! I am going to apply to college after all. I think that will be better content for my show than two middle aged people fighting over their parenting choices.

REHEARSAL DISCUSSION

1. What is Amy fighting for in this scene?

2. How can your blocking (the way you move on set) and your use of props support what you are fighting for?

3. What happened the moment before the monologue started? What do you think Amy feels at the top of the monologue?

4. Are there any lists in this speech? How can you make every item in the list standout so they don't sound the same?

5. How do Amy's parents affect her in this monologue? Let your parents' arguments affect you and react to them when they make a great point. I suggest writing in their lines and practicing this as if it was a scene.

DIRECTOR'S TIPS:

Look for the BEATS in this monologue and mark them on your script. *Beats* are shifts in *Actions*. In other words, anytime Amy switches her tactic to get what she wants, there is a BEAT change. Give each BEAT a different action, a different color. This will make your monologue come to life.

GELATO PLEASE!

Brenda Belle is an 18 year old girl from a small town in the south. For the past year, she has been working at the local ice cream shop serving locals some of the town's best ice cream flavors. Recently, her boyfriend of 6 months broke up with her after falling in love with another local girl, a coffee barista working in a nearby coffee shop. Brenda is seen talking to her co-worker, Arden, in this monologue. She is having a bad day and continues to vent her frustrations regarding life, love and people in an ice cream shop. She does so by commenting on how you can tell a person's personality by the flavor of ice cream he or she orders. Brenda wants Arden to give her hope that maybe the perfect guy is out there. The problem is, will he ever order the perfect flavor of ice cream ?

Brenda is seen handing a disheveled mother of 4 her change. The mom's 4 young children are loud, rambunctious and are already making a mess at a nearby table while enjoying their ice cream. Brenda is doing her best to stay calm, patient and professional.

Here you go... one dollar and twenty five cents *(Hands the mother her change)*. Thank you for coming to Ice Cream Heaven. *(To Arden)* Arden, want to know what the funny thing about our job is? I am able to tell what a person's personality is by the type of ice cream flavor they order. It's a skill one gets from working here countless hours, day after day. And just so you know, I will never accept another date from a guy until I learn what ice cream flavor he chooses. It will save me from a whole lot of trouble in the future. Yes, I did see Lindsay's instagram. Our favorite little coffee barista floozy is now posting daily pics of her and my idiot ex! I mean it's not hard enough that she works one block down and used to be my friend, but now she is broadcasting it all over instagram for the world to see. I'm not being dramatic! You saw it, didn't you Arden? So yes, for the world to see! Hashtag insensitive, Hashtag Coffee Baristas cannot be trusted!

But I should have known. Robert ordered Chocolate Mousse Royal when I first met him. Anyone who orders Chocolate Mousse Royal thinks they are worthy of everyone and everything. They will make you work for them. I should comment on Miss Instagram's photo and say: *"Good Luck."* Huh? I'm not being ridiculous. Look at that mother and her kids that I just served. Okay, so the little girl with the brown hair and bangs sitting down quietly, she ordered Green Tea Ice Cream. No surprise that she is the quietest out of all the children. She is eating neatly and slowly. Now check out the boy, the one the mother keeps saying "STOP ANTHONY" to. Little Anthony is kicking the chairs, making spit balls out of napkins, which by the way, you and I will have the pleasure of cleaning up, and he is allowing his melted ice cream to drip everywhere. What do you think little Anthony ordered? Wild N Reckless Sherbet of course! Need I say more? And the one with the pink hair… she ordered Mint Chocolate Chip. She has done nothing but fight with her mother the whole time. And you remember what we said about Mint

Chocolate Chip people. Exactly! Argumentative. She is the rebellious teen. And finally, the little boy who is trying to be like his brother, the kicking and crazy wild Anthony, but doesn't have it in him. Instead, he prefers to play with mommy's beautiful long hair. What do you think he ordered? Cotton Candy!

(Bridgette notices someone coming in from a far.) Oh my God! Arden, look who's coming in? That's Jason Boyd. I have had the biggest crush on him for like forever. He moved out of this town a year ago to pursue music in Nashville. He is so hot! Even hotter than I remembered. Does my hair look okay?

(Jason walks in. To Jason)

Hey Jason! Welcome to Ice Cream Heaven! What could I get for you? Oh you just want to sample some flavors. Of course you can. Welcome back. How long are you here for? The entire summer! How cool. What would you like to sample first? Vanilla! Sure. *(She hands him a spoon of the vanilla and talks to Arden)* Vanilla means he's boring. He won't go with that flavor. He is way too hot to be boring. *(To Jason)* Here's the chocolate. *(To Arden)* Chocolate means he is flirtatious, which is fun in the beginning, but not when he is your boyfriend. Please don't choose chocolate! (To Jason) Not feeling it? Great! What next? Rocky Road! Here you go. *(To Arden)* If he goes with this one, it means he's aggressive and motivated. I like the goal oriented part, but the aggression in a relationship can often lead to a lot of fights. So, this is not the perfect flavor. *(To Jason)* No. Not that one? What else would you like to try? Coffee it is! (To Arden) Coffee guys are passionate. Which is great in the moment, but then after awhile, it takes a lot to keep them stimulated. Please say no to the coffee Jason. (To Jason) No coffee. Phew! How about you try one more? Here's the Pralines and Cream. *(To Arden)* This is a good flavor. Guys who choose this tend to be supportive and don't need the spotlight. But Jason is born to be in the spotlight. This is definitely not his flavor. Hmmm. Should I be worried that he can't decide? This is not looking so good. (to Jason) What was that? Gelato? We don't serve any gelato, I'm so sorry. Yeah. It was nice seeing you too. *(Jason begins to leave, but Bridgette quickly stops him)* Wait! Jason, would you like me to show you where the nearest gelato cafe is? Yes, I would love to join you. I love Gelato! Give me a moment and I will meet you outside.

(To Arden) Gelato! He ordered Gelato! So?! Are you crazy? Do you know what this means, Arden? It means he is not willing to settle. He will do whatever it takes to get what he wants, and what he wants is a sophisticated, unique, worldly woman like *moi*. He is not into just anyone or anything, like some floozy coffee barista. Jason is into Gelato! He ordered the perfect flavor! Yes, I know Gelato is not a flavor, but you know what I mean. Here's my apron Arden. Take over for me... please. I need to get some Gelato with Jason Boyd!

REHEARSAL DISCUSSION:

1. What kind of a monologue is this? In your own words, describe this piece and the overall style and tone of it.

2. Describe the relationship Brenda has will all the other characters in the scene. Also, explain in detail what her relationships are to any events mentioned, any other characters mentioned, and the setting and objects in it.

3. What are 3 facts you learned about Brenda from this monologue? What are three conclusions you can come up with regarding Brenda's personality based on these facts?

4. Would you say this monologue is a comedy? Why or why not?

5. What emotions or feelings is Brenda experiencing in this monologue? What physical actions can you use to extend the emotions she is feeling?

DIRECTOR'S TIP:

Anytime Brenda realizes what she is fighting for is not going well, take on an entirely different tone.

THE PROM DRESS

Tammy is a 17 year old store clerk at a formal gown shop. At the start of the monologue, Tammy is seen happy. She looks hopeful and inspired! In this monologue, she is talking to her friend and co-worker, Coco.

Coco, it's May 1st… the start of Prom Season, and that makes me happy! This place is gonna be packed with wishful teens all dreaming about the best night of senior year- PROM NIGHT. And you and I get to help them pick out the most important dress of their life…The Prom Gown! Coco, you're just being negative! Come on! Let's turn a new page together in our life starting today! We are both getting prom dates. We still have a month!

(Tammy's mood suddenly shifts.) Why would you bring Bobby up when you know I'm finally over him? I'm no longer going to spend my beautiful energy trying to figure out why the man I loved for almost a year, broke up with me when he saw that I used the B word- BOYFRIEND, on INSTAGRAM. Warning to all single ladies… never post a picture of you and your man on National Boyfriend's Day if you want your relationship to work. Ugh…I'm so over him! Coco, I'm ready to meet a man who knows my worth and can say the word: GIRLFRIEND!

(Tammy sees someone walk in and it causes her to freeze. She panics.)

Oh my God! I don't believe it. Coco, hide! Just hide! Why?
Because look who just walked in! The new girl Bobby dates,
Beyonka. He must have asked her to prom! This can't be
true! He has only been with her for 3 weeks. Oh my God. I
can't breathe! Coco, I can't breathe. *(Trying to catch her breath
before she has a full blown panic attack)* Okay, okay you got this
Tammy. Mind over Body! *(Takes in deep breaths and exhales
them out with intention.)* Coco, this is what I want you to do.
If you are truly my best friend, you are going to get that
ugly gown we were trying to get rid of and sell it to her!
If she is going to the prom with my Bobby, it is our job to
find her the ugliest dress ever! I'll just be waiting over here
and if somehow I collapse, hit my head and die, will you
tell Bobby for me that I HATE HIM! Tell him I absolutely
HATE HIS GUTS and HOPE HE LIVES UNHAPPILY
EVER AFTER.

*(Coco walks away and Tammy observes the whole scene, talking to
herself.)*

Look at her! She's bossing her friend around as if she
is someone important. You are a senior going to prom,
not the *frickin'* Queen of England! Good girl Coco! Yes,
convince her that she'll look beautiful in that dress. I hope
she can get her big hips in it! The friend knows it's ugly, but
she wouldn't dare say. *(Beyonka gets into the dress.)* She's in it!
Go ahead Beyonka, look at yourself in the mirror long and
hard, because if you really knew Bobby the way I know
him, there is no way you'd be getting that dress! He'd hate

it. He would want a tight and sexy gown, not a girl who looks like a cupcake!

(Coco comes back) So did she buy it? Good job! You really are a good sales woman Coco! *(Tammy breaks into tears.)* She is going to look awful in that dress. I don't need a tissue! I'm fine! Oh, who am I kidding! Even if she does have the ugliest dress in the store, she still gets to go to prom with Bobby! Maybe May 1st is not so hopeful after all! Wake me up when Prom Season is over!

REHEARSAL DISCUSSION:

1. How would you compare the feelings Tammy experiences in the beginning of the monologue to how she feels at the end?

2. Have you ever had a broken heart? Who broke your heart? Describe the feelings you experienced and go back to the day your heart was first broken. Where were you? What time of day was it? Who was there? Write it down.

3. Who is Tammy talking to in this monologue? How would you describe Tammy's relationship with her?

4. What does Tammy want in this monologue?

5. What or who is in her way of getting it?

DIRECTOR'S TIP:

Pay attention to your focal points in this monologue and be clear and consistent regarding where they are. For instance, when Tammy is talking to Coco, where is Coco? When Beyonka walks in, how are you going to establish this in your space and make the audience believe this is actually happening? Plot out your space and then rehearse this by making it come to life.

THE PROMISE RING

Blake, a senior in high school, is heart broken because Anna, his college girlfriend, no longer wants to date him anymore.

You are not that into me anymore? Yes you are Anna! You are! You just must be tired from all the homework you're getting in college. I am in love with you Anna. Look, I gave you a promise ring! A promise ring! And you accepted it! You seemed to be madly in love with me this summer too! And now you go away to college and forget all about me? Is it because I am still a senior in high school?

I know I should have told you I was coming up to see you, but you never answered any of my calls. I was only texting you at 1 AM because I saw you were out. No, I do not stalk your instagram and Snapchat. But what do you expect? Nothing new is happening for me in high school, except for the fact that I miss you! Anna, don't you miss me too? Answer me! Controlling? Your therapist said I was controlling? You should stop seeing her then. I know I was the one who told you to go to her in the first place, but it was a bad idea. *(Blake sees Anna's phone blink.)* Who is John and why he is he texting you? I am not snooping at your phone, but it's blinking like crazy. Let me see the texts if this John is just a friend! Why won't you let me see it? I am not going crazy, I am in love!

You can't break up with me. You accepted my promise ring. Wow, how can you just throw it at me and walk away like that. What kind of girl are you! HEARTLESS? No, I didn't mean that. You have the biggest heart in the world. Oh my God, what am I going to do without you Anna? Please come back! I will change! I swear, just come back!

REHEARSAL DISCUSSION:

1. What is this monologue about? Explain it in own your words.

2. How probable is the behavior of the characters? Can you relate to this in anyway? How?

3. How does Blake's emotions change from Beginning, Middle to End? Title each section specifying how Blake shifts from emotion to emotion when he does not get what he wants.

4. Why does Anna want to break up with Blake?

5. How would you describe Blake's and Anna's relationship before Anna took off for college? Why do you think she accepted the promise ring?

DIRECTOR'S TIP:

Turn this monologue into a scene. Write in Anna's lines. Then rehearse it with a partner, repeating the last phrase of your partner's line before you say your next one. How does repeating what your partner says affect your next line? Then, rehearse the monologue without your partner, taking in Anna and letting her affect you.

WHERE IS GOD?

Mila/Mark, a high school student struggles to understand why bad things happen.

I used to go to church every Sunday and say my prayers. I truly believed in God, and no matter what happened to me, I could always find peace in knowing that God was there. But now I am not even sure that there is a God. If there was a God, then why would he allow so many students in my school to get shot by one disturbed teenager?

That day was beyond a nightmare. I was never so scared in my life and I kept praying to God for the kid to stop shooting, but the more I prayed…the more gun shots there were. I shivered under my desk, rolled into a ball, and held onto to the handles of my chair for dear life praying to stay alive.

I was one of the few lucky ones he did not shoot. Why did God spare me, but take my best friend Brian? How will I ever go back to school again and feel safe? Where was God that day? I'm so sick of people saying that incidents like this bring us closer together and make us stronger! Give me a break! They say that because they don't know what else to say. I mean, how can we ever move on? We can't!

REHEARSAL DISCUSSION:

1. Why is this monologue titled: "Where is God?"

2. Who do you think Mila/Mark is talking to? What does she/he want from him/her?

3. How will your character connect the past with the present? Are they telling a past story in order to find something now?

4. What does this monologue say about life? What is the message?

5. What issues are raised? Write 1 sentence to summarize what this monologue is about.

DIRECTOR'S TIP:

This is a painful monologue to perform, as this is a real, scary issue that today's students face. To connect to this piece authentically, I suggest you research the experience of students who experienced gun violence at school.

I'M SCREWED

Steve is in big trouble! He discovers that one of the meanest, strongest guys in school wants to beat him up.

What do you mean Jerry wants to beat me up? He is a wrestler and I am a writer! What the heck could make him want to beat me up? I didn't even know he knew I existed.

This is a joke, right Richie? Oh my God! You're not joking. You're serious! Jerry Hansen wants to beat me up! What am I going to do? Do you even know why? Because he saw me talking to his girlfriend! That's crazy!

Diane is in my science class and the teacher paired us to be lab partners. I have to talk to her. Jerry saw me blushing in class? Well, Diane is pretty, so I cannot help myself from blushing. You can't control a blush!

When is he planning to beat me up? Tomorrow at lunch? Wonderful! Richie, what am I going to do? Are you going to help me?

REHEARSAL DISCUSSION:

1. Who are the characters mentioned in this monologue? How would you describe each one?

2. What does Steve want from Richie? What is his obstacle?

3. Have you ever been in a situation where someone wanted to beat you up? How did you react?

4. Do you agree with Steve that you cannot control a blush?

5. Why does Steve think Richie is joking at first?

DIRECTOR'S TIP:

Do not only speak Steve's words, but allow his thoughts to make his words believable. What is his inner monologue? Write it out.

THE GENIE

Cole is so excited that the cast list for the school musical has finally been posted. He runs into the school building with his best friend Patricia to read it.

It's finally up! I'm so excited, but also so nervous so I am not even sure I can look. Why don't you look first, because if I'm not on it, I'm going to freak out. Ever since I could remember, I wanted to be cast as The Genie in "Aladdin." I have been preparing myself for this role my whole life, so I beg you, look for me. I just can't do it.

Wait! Don't look yet. What about if we go for a snack first and then come back? Okay, okay, you're right. I must calm down. I just hope that Miss Joanne recognizes talent when she sees it. Okay…I am ready for you to look. Ahhhh…this is so nerve wracking!!!

(Patricia looks at the list) I cannot tell by the look on your face if I was cast or not. Patricia say something! Oh my God, you're congratulating me! That means I got it? I got the part? What? I was cast as Aladdin? But I don't want to be Aladdin. How dare Miss Joanne! Aladdin? I am so much better than that! Who was cast as the Genie? YOU! This has to be a mistake. How could you do this to me? Of course you're at fault. You never even liked "Aladdin." You wanted them to do *"Beauty and The Beast"* this year. You

should have never auditioned. You destroyed my dream. I am too talented to be in a school play anyway. I quit!

REHEARSAL DISCUSSION:

1. How is the setting, where and when this monologue takes place, affecting the action and conflict?

2. What is the conflict in this monologue?

3. Why is Cole so angry that he was cast as Aladdin?

4. Do you agree that Cole should quit the play? Why or why not?

5. What role have you always wanted to play? How would you feel if your friend got the part instead of you?

DIRECTOR'S TIP:

Find similarities in yourself that align with Cole. Write them down and then use them in your performance.

TOO SHY

Keith is explaining to his buddy Scott why he cannot go to the School's homecoming dance.

Nothing is wrong with me! I just don't want to go to homecoming this year. Besides, I don't even know how to dance, so what's the point? I have some studying I want to get a head start on anyway. I won't regret this. Homecoming is just not that important to me.

What about Fabiana? She asked you if I was going? Yeah right! She would never ask you that. You want me to ask her out? Have you gone mad! Fabiana is one of the prettiest, nicest, smartest girls in school, I'm sure she's already got a date. She doesn't? How do you know all this? You asked her? Great, and now you are trying to get me to ask her out? That's what you've been up to. Well, what if I ask her out and she says no? Do you know how embarrassed I would be? Besides, I am too shy to talk to girls as pretty as Fabiana. I wouldn't even know what to say or what to do with my hands when I talk. Sometimes when I talk to girls, I start moving around in some of the most awkward ways, and well then I just get in my head and forget what it was I wanted to say in the first place.

Wait, did you just say Fabiana is going to ask me out? Um, um well...oh my God, when? In a few minutes? Do I look okay? How do I say yes? See, I'm no good at this. Do you think I should wink at her like this when I say yes? *(Keith shows Scott an awkward wink.)* No, that looks weird, like creepy right? Okay, now I'm really nervous. Staying home to study would just be so much easier.

REHEARSAL DISCUSSION:

1. Why is Scott telling his friend Keith to take Fabiana to the homecoming dance?

2. Do you think Keith really doesn't want to go to homecoming? Why or why not?

3. What does Keith want from Scott in this monologue? What is his obstacle?

4. Have you ever wanted to skip a school function? What function was it? Why did you want to skip it?

5. How would you describe Keith? How would you describe Scott? Do you think they are good friends? Why or why not?

DIRECTOR'S TIP:

Anytime you perform a monologue, you should be focused on *"the other person"* you are talking to. In this case, your focus should be on your friend Scott. I suggest always having a specific person in mind from your own life to talk to that could be substituted for Scott. Imagine that this person was really there and try to see their face, smile, body, and reactions. React off that person and the monologue will come to life.

MY MOTHER'S NEW BOYFRIEND

Chris confronts his/her mother for kissing a new man.

You and Dad are not even officially divorced yet! How could you be kissing another man at a restaurant where other people could see you when you are not even divorced from my father? How could you do this Mom? How could you kiss another guy? He is not Dad! Why won't you even try to work it out with Dad? Seventeen years of marriage and you're going to give up just like that? Does Dad even know you're dating? When did you even meet this jerk?

No, I'm not going to calm down! My family is falling apart and my friends and I just saw my mother kissing a man that isn't my father. And the worst part about all of this is how happy you looked. You looked happy with him. You were laughing. You looked like you loved him. I can't remember the last time you were happy with Dad and looked at him like that.

I don't want you to see that guy anymore. What do you mean that's not up to me? I'm your son. Don't you see, he's going to destroy our family. I want us to be a family again. I need that Mom. Please, don't divorce Dad. Try to work it out. Do it for me!

REHEARSAL DISCUSSION:

1. In your own words, describe what this monologue is about?

2. What is Chris experiencing in this monologue?

3. What happened the moment before this monologue took place? How do you think that affected Chris and his mom?

4. Do you think Chris' mom will try to work on her marriage with his father? Why or why not?

5. Can you relate to how Chris is feeling in this monologue? Why or why not? Explain.

DIRECTOR'S TIP:

Chris just experienced a painful moment in his life. Recall a painful moment in your life that caused you to become hysterical with someone you love. Relive every detail of it, and then try performing your monologue immediately after.